T0069180

Freeways & Aqueducts

ALSO BY JAMES HARMS

Quarters
The Joy Addict
Modern Ocean

Freeways & Aqueducts

poems by
James Harms

Carnegie Mellon University Press
Pittsburgh 2004

Acknowledgments

Grateful acknowledgment is made to the editors of the following magazines, where some of these poems first appeared, occasionally in different form:

American Literary Review ("Twilight at the Edge of the Empire"), *Antietam Review* ("Aubade in Morgantown"), *Caffeine Destiny* ("June"), *Chelsea* ("Winter Memory of Summer Trespass"), *Crazyhorse* ("Lucy," "When the Circus Comes"), *The Gettysburg Review* ("Reunion of Extra Shadows," "The Sanity of My Vessel"), *Luna* ("Midwinter Visitant," "Want"), *The Missouri Review* ("Elegy as Evening, as Exodus," "In Any Country," "Mother to Daughter"), *Natural Bridge* ("Loves Leaves More than Flowers"), *Pleiades* ("Pacific Standard Time"), *Poetry* ("Sleek for the Long Flight"), *Poetry International* ("California Stars in West Virginia (for Walt)," "Copernicus," "Never Mind," "Photo of My Stepfather in an Altadena Evening"), *Poetry Northwest* ("Los Angeles, the Angels"), *Sycamore Review* ("Farmers Market, Los Angeles"), *Tamaqua* ("Instead of Nothing"), *TriQuarterly* ("Union Station, Los Angeles (the Reagan Years)"), *West Branch* ("By Heart," "Harriet Doerr," "Western Sky").

The ten poems in the sequence "L.A. Afterglow" appeared as a chapbook in *The Idaho Review*. My thanks to Mitch Wieland.

"Los Angeles, the Angels" was reprinted in the *1999 Pushcart Prize XXIII*.

My thanks to the Eberly College of Arts and Sciences at West Virginia University for its generous support.

Design by Linda Warren
Printed by Westcott Press

Contents

TO WALT AND PHOEBE

They were right, my dear, all those voices were right
And still are; this land is not the sweet home that it looks,
    Nor its peace the historical calm of a site
Where something was settled once and for all ...

–W.H. Auden

I discover the light of a place gradually,
and only through painting it.

–Richard Diebenkorn

ONE: WEST

...Fifty yards further up the beach, a boy carrying swim fins walked out of the waves and headed for the steps. She supposed he was Mrs. Scott's grandson, aged about sixteen, lean of build and badly sunburned, his wet hair plastered to his face. Elizabeth saw him smile as he came near. Then his happiness spilled over, and he spoke.

"How about this?" he said. "How about it?" Turning, he lifted his hand to the sky, the shore, the water, her.

−Harriet Doerr, from "Like Heaven"

Los Angeles, The Angels

Doves love a dying palm. They nestle in the loud fronds.
        They hum
and shiver. The way days end here: no click; no door sealing in
        the light.
The way dusk enters the room and embitters it; the way
the paint absorbs its shadows, the skin absorbing stares.

I hear you and I hate it. I hate hearing your voice in the leaves
as I sand down the bureau; I drag out the furniture, drag it out   *
onto the driveway but still, *How have you come so far*
without belief? I rake the yard to muffle your voice.

Evening is slithering toward me, and behind it, believe me,
the cold. Night is a chance to see the stars as they were
when Greeks in their shifts and leather slippers, their
gruesome beards sandy and caked with salt—before turning
toward each other to sleep—listened, terrified, to the laughter
breaking with the waves, the slim sheet of water drawing close.

And their dreams were worn as singlets in the next day's race,
the cloth of sleep sewn into waking, the long day of sleep.
Because they knew, as I have chosen not to—each turn at the wheel
a chance to drive my purchases and children to a clear spot
on the hillside—they knew what we would become: old thieves
in beaten-up cars, idling at the signals, skin going bad in the sun.

Night is a wind blowing away the light, which streaks and burns
on its way west. Night is an empty lung, and here's the moon:
the armoire mounts a broken dresser; the lawn grows plastic chairs.   13
How can I forgive you? How have you come so far? I rake
the dark shards from the grass, your voice in pieces, *so far, belief.*

Western Sky

Lazarus could never remember
which pocket he put his hand in
when those crowding around
asked to see the holes, mistaking him
for someone else.
And the many melding lights of Los Angeles
are visible from the moon, or so
says my friend at JPL, who should know:
he mans the telescope on Mt. Wilson,
which stares these days at a dropped ceiling.
Nevertheless, it sees; it is like
closing your eyes and watching
the flecks of dream
leftover from the night before.
My friend spends
his nights alone looking
for what? He can't say.
It seems we all want
to see new worlds, the planet nearest
the silver star, the frozen sun.
We all want to know it didn't hurt,
the sentence slipped like a burning cigarette
into someone's ear, how the once
best friend declares his love for whom
you loved and it doesn't hurt. After all,
it's always better to know, though
how much longer do we expect to live?
And will it sear and scar, this new knowledge,
will it join the other blue marks not fading from sight,
those strange hard shadows,
not wrinkles or lines exactly
but fossil traces of every sweet truth, as if
we could ever learn and let it go?
When Lazarus asked for water someone said,
"Tell us first your story, my friend, then drink."

Here was proof that the body endures—
thirsty or not we go on,
though how quiet and cool it had been
he said, and how very much
he now needed water. And when finally
allowed to die, he rose swiftly
and saw how the oceans shaped
the slivers of land, how they lit
the world a warm soft blue, as if
a family had gone to bed forgetfully,
leaving the television on, its light
a little fuzzy behind the curtains.

The Episcopal Minister

At the dinner table alone
after midnight, my father is back
from the hospital, back
from the residence for retired Episcopalians,
the row of convalescent homes
on Fair Oaks Boulevard, the houses
above the Rose Bowl where the rich
insist, back from bedsides
and kitchen tables, from sadness
so vast it empties the rooms of air,
back from confessions, from numbered breaths.
Like every other night he has prayed
with the dying and infirmed, held hands
so weak they slip from his own
whenever he thinks of where
he'd rather be. Like every other night
he has tacked to the blue edge of evening
a string of visits, the hours after
closing the books on the church school,
finishing the sermon, writing notes
to benefactors and bishops.
He is home for dinner, a few glasses
of burgundy, alone in darkness
in the rectory's enormous dining room,
the table set for one a few hours ago
by my mother, who has been asleep
since ten. In the rooms above him:
two girls, two boys, his wife and a collie,
only the dog aware that he is home.
He sips the wine, feels the light
on his face and hands, the light through
blinds left open, a street lamp
on Altadena Boulevard the only moon
for miles, the L.A. sky a neon-fogged mirror.

Two deodars and a redwood,
a lawn of ragged St. Augustine
separate the house from the street.
He listens for everything, for anything, hears
a car turn at the corner, hears it coast
down Maiden Lane idling
in the throes of gravity. Beneath the engine
noise is another sound, the rustle of wings.
A note is pinned to the placemat,
"Spaghetti in the fridge," and he'll rise
in just a minute, he'll eat the dish cold,
watch out the window for owl shadows
on the driveway, so certain he is
of what he thinks he saw the night before,
the great birds passing back and forth
in the limbs high above the house,
he is certain they were birds.
If he wished he could walk out and stand
beneath the evergreens, he could watch
the owls exchange places in the trees;
he could let the calico out for a late night chance
to do its business, watch it vanish from the lawn
beneath a rushing shadow. If he wished
but he doesn't wish. They were birds,
there is no doubt of it. He hears
the collie start its slow descent;
it's time to get the food from the fridge,
it's what the dog has dragged
its tired body downstairs for; every night
he lowers his plate to the floor to let it
finish his dinner. He pours another glass,
sees his hand ignite in the streetlight
through the window, pulls it back into
shadow, lays it bare again.
Above him his wife, the children, the owls.
He is certain of it. And here's the dog,
right here. Good boy.

Elegy as Evening, as Exodus

North of Malibu

The Pacific is nothing like its name.
For one thing, there are no silences,
despite the palm trees leaning into stillness.

Poppies rise like fire from the chaparral
on the bluffs, the manzanita, the oil in its leaves.
And every few yards a stubborn yucca,

late blossoms struggling to catch up at the edge
of whatever, this modern earth, tectonic rafts
slipping north and west, the ocean torn into white lace.

Tan knees tucked beneath my chin,
tan knees like a boy's, I sat watch
through the afternoon, staring at the islands:

Anacapa, San Miguel, Catalina to the south.
I heard a phone ring, a buoy bell, sun dissolving
into sea. I heard a name escape its word,

the wind between waves. The islands were rose and gray
in the last light of a last Tuesday,
the rock around me dark and trembling, volcanic.

I sat in the splash zone, black urchins
tucked into wet crevices at my feet,
a keyhole limpet next to my left hand.

And though you would suppose the islands
would vanish into the channel when the sun did,
for hours I could see their shapes, like whales

sleeping peacefully on the horizon,
like ships. Ships waiting for enough light,
for safe passage, for cargo. For all of us.

Lucy

I hadn't seen her in three years
when she showed up one afternoon
in my driveway, a son
in her arms. An hour later
she said it was too soon
to kiss again, too soon.
We were standing in the kitchen
doorway—she had just come
to say hello and now we were
saying good-bye, so I tried again.
She tucked her chin into her blouse,
shifted Stephen over her hip,
who slept but held a dirty nest
he'd found in my mother's hibiscus,
grey twigs woven with the down
of dried grass, slips of bright thread
carried from the schoolyard across
the street, a few shards of foil
picked from the neighbor's garbage.
Mockingbirds build carefully
from whatever is convenient
and close by, then hector anyone
or thing who comes too close.
But we'd seen only swallows
in the rotten fence posts, the low eaves
of the church next door. No mockingbirds.
No parrots. I told her about the parrots.
A pet shop nearby burned down
in the 30s, and even now they returned
to our great eucalyptus, pet parrots
gone wild. She didn't believe me,
wouldn't kiss me, couldn't stay.
And when she said, "I have to go,"
her face gave a little
around the eyes and mouth,

as if the slim bones that held
it all in place were falling inward.
She believed in Jesus so much
it hurt her to look at her little boy,
whose father, a black man—a man
she could never have imagined loving
four years ago, when I'd asked her
over lunch one day which of our friends
she could see herself with and she said,
"No, not Ronny," and I asked why
and she told me, "He's black"—
Stephen's father had loved her
just enough to give her Stephen
but not enough to stay.
They hadn't married, she said,
and she had forgiven him.
When she looked at her little boy
it happened again: her face slipped,
as if a seam had torn but not quite
given way. "I have to go," she said.
She wouldn't let me kiss her.
And when she left, little Stephen
woke up to wave. From his car seat
in the back of her neighbor's Dodge,
the car she'd borrowed to visit me,
Stephen did what his mother said.
He waved. From where I stood
it looked like he was trying to shake
the nest out of his hand, but he was
just waving, bits of string and grass
flying off. I knew that a good part
of that nest would end up in Lucy's hair,
that she would put Stephen down
for his nap and sit at the mirror,
brush out the nest with one hand
and touch her face over and over
with a single finger, as if surprised
to find that, after so long,
it was all beginning to show.

Pacific Standard Time

I like what's on at nine and you don't,
but you sit with me anyway because it's cool
in the den, and the dishes are done,
and your show's at ten, and the laundry
can wait. So I lean into your lap and let you
rest your hand on my head. I get sort of
pissed at your giggles, the dumb jokes
I don't get, but it doesn't matter; you'll tell
them all again tomorrow over coffee
and toast, so I sleep through most of it.

~

You start to move, to slide yourself out
from under my head saying, *Hey, it's time*;
I wake and watch you take the fan upstairs.
I think of when I asked you earlier
what I should get to go with Zinfandel
and you said, *Why don't you buy us a life?*
then threw me a twenty. I can feel
the change in my pocket.
You're back downstairs, loading the dishwasher.
It's time, you say again, and I suppose it is.

~

I move through the rooms pulling shades
and shutting lights. You're at the head
of the stairs with floss hanging from your mouth.
Would you bring up my magazine, you say,
It's on the kitchen table. I sit for a few
flipping through the pages, until I find one
turned down, an ad for Jamaica, then another,
a woman with a towel around her head,
her toe nails painted "Acetylene Red." And finally,
a guy in shorts smoking a filterless cigarette.

~

It's where you want to be, what you wish
you looked like, what I guess you'd see
if I were more like the me I used to be.
I leave the magazine on the table,
I'll say it wasn't there. And when
you come down on your own to find it
you'll wonder what I'm up to. But by then
I'll be gone, somewhere you've never been,
fast asleep, snoring. I'll make sure
you never find me, even with a map of dreams.

Farmers Market, Los Angeles

Bob was accused of baldness
at his tenth reunion, though none
of his good friends had noticed;
we'd been there all along
so the slow thinning never registered—
one minute the sugar maple's laughing
in the breeze, shaking its hands
like a little girl in a bus station bathroom,
towels all gone and the blower busted,
the next we're cold, listening
to bones click near the eaves.
On 3rd and Fairfax
the pushcart vendors park
in a row facing the tour buses
and argue about prices;
even the independents
want to join the cartel.
And though it's tough to find
popsicles or black licorice,
the Guatemalan shaved ice
and sugared coconut are less
than a buck. Bob's sampling
the fried banana and nodding,
licking his fingers. He looks
better than ever, his waist
a spring sapling still tied to a pole.
Dwayne and I are talking while we walk
through the Market, not watching
where we're going, stepping into hats
as though they're puddles of old pennies,
waiting for the first warm day
when we can shuck our winter shoes
and feel the copper between our toes.

And here comes Bob
carrying a papier mache donkey
that even from here, across
the parking lot, we can tell
is filled with candy. One thing
about Bob, he's tall and never
wears a hat (I guess that's two things),
and when he's smiling you can see him for miles.
He's smiling I think—yes,
there it is. Holding the donkey
out in front of him like a lantern,
he's smiling on his way to join us.
We'll toss a rope into the trees and
catch the other end, string it up high
while each of us, blindfolded and blissed,
swings a bat at that donkey.

Reunion of Extra Shadows

Burger Continental, Pasadena, California

Jeff brings the fries. His little boy carries ketchup.
Chewing softly a sprig of ginger
to settle her stomach, my sister
fills a beer mug with sun tea and sugar.
She's due in May, her second, a boy to play
with Daddy, who's watching the races
on a TV tucked in the corner.
Matt's lifting his shirt,
the scar disappearing into his trousers,
sparrows in the ivy,
the ivy spilling down the courtyard wall, the rain . . .
the rain's a happy memory, green gloves
on a dying elm. Where's Toby? Where's Eric?

Ralph is watching the west entrance.
John is talking to him. Before the pigeons
ruined the *Campari* umbrellas,
this was the place to lunch *al fresco*.
Someone spills the pitcher of water.
Bob throws Melissa a wad of napkins.
The box of impatiens along the wall beneath
the ivy, an August from childhood:
wet January, cool June, poppies on the foothills.
Listen, John says. No, listen. Bob snaps
a rubberband, the pigeons jump.
Dwayne disappears.

Jeff sings a Buffalo Tom song to Amy,
who's saying, Who? Who? until our own Tom
stands to make a toast, to all us "owls
and former derelicts," and we all say,
Who? as if we've never, as if we've never.

"I hear she's nearly tired of him, that she's—
wait . . . here she comes."
Over goes another glass.
The management here loves us despite
the years of wrecked linen,
the tooth Alan lost in the bathroom.
Where's Alan? Dwayne returns with more beer.

I'm the driver, says Matt,
a rain of wadded napkins . . .
the rain, the lupine like bits of sky
scattered through the hills, the fires
next month, maybe never. Ronny strolls
through the iron gateway without Blake,
though he's pulling an extra shadow.
Come to think of it, we all are.

Loves Leaves More than Flowers

There's a touch that isn't touch but something
less, less than breath or a breeze through an orchard,
less than the white petal on Annemarie's eyelash

as she walks up with a turtle in her small hands.
"It crawled under the fence," she says, and she taps

the shell and hums to where its head should be,
pulls a myrtle leaf from her pocket and explains to me:
"God loves leaves more than flowers."

Her handful of God begins to poke out its head
and legs, swims a bit in her palm, chews the leaf.

And though nothing calls to me from the potted fuchsia,
nothing from the lilies swarming a rainwarped fence
(a fence of redwood patched with pine),

and though wearing his disguise of two scrub jays
and a blossoming almond tree, wearing like an old

bandanna the pale blue sky torn with mare's tails,
God, it seems, is nearby waiting, as always, for prayer.
My lips move just ahead of thought as I watch

Annie slip the turtle back beneath the fence.
I listen to pigeons in the almond trees, the rustle

of wings or wind sorting through blossoms,
my voice like a bit of dust falling with sunlight,
something or someone looking for leaves.

Copernicus

I didn't handle it well, a sudden friendship
in the Copernicus Room high above San Francisco
with a beautician from Stockton. She was in town visiting
her father, whose left leg had been removed at the knee.
"Diabetes," she said. "What are you having?"

We sat and watched the bay darken like an angry face,
talked over drinks about his stubborn refusal
to give up cigarettes, how he kept his extra shoe
on the nightstand beside his bed. And then,
like a severed head, sincerity made its appearance,

scaring the hell out of both of us. I didn't intend
to tell her that my father was whole but absent
("wholly absent?" she said), or that I'd dreamt
for years—a recurring nightmare—of slicing off my hand
while spreading mustard on a piece of bread.

"What kind of bread?" she said. The light began to change
just then, the strange copper light that seems to smother
the headlands before passing from Alcatraz to Angel Island,
a fast retreating shadow we stopped talking to watch,
sunlight traveling toward us, then vanishing. The fog

closed off the bay, left the bridge a pair of rusty towers,
cables dropping into silence, a silence that seemed
solid as stone, a cliff of chalcedony. I imagined the clouds
stiffening like egg whites, a confectioner's dream
creeping slowly toward the city. And how do we measure

the world, I thought, with what we see, or what we know
is there? "Another beer, please," she said, "and some nuts."
She was ordering for me, pulling her chair a little closer.
"Look there," she said tapping the glass. Forty floors down
and two miles out, a small tug had popped free of the fog

29

and was chugging toward a circle of sunlight on the bay,
the one spot of bright water. She held her breath
until it got there, then broke into applause.
"He made it!" she said, and drained away her rum and coke,
patted my arm and picked her purse off the floor.

"You'll never hurt anyone," she said, but I didn't get it.
"Your dream ... You're scared you're going to hurt someone,
it's a symbol." Then she scooped the ashtray—made of flesh red
carnelian—off the table into her purse. "A souvenir," she said,
and left. My beer arrived a few minutes later,

along with a fresh bowl of nuts. It was the Carnelian Room
I later learned, when I told my sister what had happened,
not Copernicus. "CarNEELian," she said, as if what mattered—
as if what I needed to get right—was where I'd been.

Harriet Doerr

Harriet Doerr lives in Pasadena, where I was born
in 1960 in St. Luke's Hospital on Altadena Drive.
If you drive north on Altadena along the canyon,
then take the sweeping curve west past
the mansions with their lawns of deep St. Augustine,
you'll arrive, eventually, at the Lake Avenue
intersection, where each August in the parking lot
next to the Albertsons supermarket the circus appeared,
like a sudden set of sails blown magically into the harbor.
Five blocks north, on Las Flores Street, on the grounds
of the old Kellog mansion, the peacocks screamed
late into the night, dusting the tops of the deodars
with their long feathers, the iron gates with their script so
familiar from cereal boxes. In "Edie: A Life," an English-
woman arrives in Pasadena to raise five half-orphaned children.
No where in the story is Pasadena mentioned, but in 1919,
in California, where else? I wish Harriet Doerr
would write one more story about the forgetfulness
of children, especially those who molt slyly in the corners
and leave their old bodies behind like perfect little sacks
to be collected and stored. Each year the sack is a little
larger, until at last they make a sort of nesting doll,
the largest as big as a casket and nearly like the person
the child will become. Nearly. In "Edie," the children
forget for years, then remember in time to say Goodbye,
though Edie isn't listening, her face turned to the window,
toward the memory of the sun in the night sky. The gardens
of Pasadena are old and thick with roses, with nasturtiums
and morning glories, arbors of bougainvillea, the small groves
of orange trees and kumquats: Harriet Doerr must remember
so much as she sits in her garden waiting. If it is a particularly
smoggy day, as it usually is in July or August, she might
wear a white, gauze surgeon's mask, as she did in 1918
when the flu finally reached California: five delicate
white veils for each school day in a week.

In the canyons off Altadena Drive, the mountain lions
have returned; a hiker is now and then taken; there is
poison oak on the hillsides; rattlesnakes coil on the sun-
warmed rocks. And the eucalyptus near the streams.
And the poppies everywhere, sage furring the hillsides,
yucca and manzanita and everything that so easily burns.
Harriet Doerr is waiting in her garden listening
to the oleander. If it is Wednesday before nine she might
hear the garbage truck, the men laughing as they lift
the trash cans and shake loose their contents. I know
I will never again live in the shadow of Mt. Wilson
beneath the blind telescope; I will never again hike
into the hills from the firebreak above Loma Alta, fall
asleep beneath a black oak in Eaton Canyon as the foothills
redden with sunset. And Harriet Doerr will never again
watch that same sunset fool the rangers into thinking
fire, so vividly the yellow sage takes on the blush of dusk.
But she will remember it. In "Like Heaven," memory
is too much a part of longing to really help. Rather,
it's a child's helpless happiness in the surf at sunset
that ignites the actual, the full body of joy. And so the sack
that once held happiness, filled now with nothing more
than love for the sack itself, is a cruel sort of joke, though
necessary. How badly, it seems, we need to be forgotten.

Photo of My Stepfather in an Altadena Evening

There is only one picture of Gene
that stills the sadness long enough
for me to see it. He sits
on a piece of patio furniture in a shirt
aswarm with blue and gray fish,
slumped slightly as if settling in
before stiffening his spine against
the chair's rubber straps.
There is a streak of shadow
slanting through the frame
and dusting his hair with darkness,
as if the evening at the edges of the photo
is swelling with time,
is rinsing away the years as well as the light.
But there is little gray in Gene's hair,
which even now is clay-colored
and fine, as it's been as long
as I've known him. Unlike my father
or mother, I remember not knowing him,
an empty sleeve attached to a jacket,
which hangs in the hall closet
of a house long sold.
Gene has never listened
to Frank Sinatra or Johnny Mathis.
He has never asked to throw a baseball
with me, for which I am grateful.
The one time I saw him finger a satin shirt
was a moment I imagined as I ordered tuxedos
for my groomsmen, my father
and for him. He stood close to my mother
through the service like a birch
leaning slightly toward the clearing
where the sun strikes first
before spreading to the woods.

For twenty years he took all the pictures.
Which is why there is only one
of the sadness stilled, the patio cooling
and Gene at rest in the play of light
and shadow at afternoon's end, the edge
of evening. Perhaps
he is beside my mother now
in their new house near Modesto,
in the kitchen I'm sure, the windows open
to almond trees, the muffled noise
of branches budding. They seem
to be listening to the threads
giving way in the earth,
the soft rip of dahlias pushing up.
But no. It's music in the living room
they hear, Beethoven I would bet, the sadness
of air blended into song,
a wordless story the two of them
have heard so often they know enough
to stop, to turn toward each other
against the steady pull
of the earth, which spins as always
in the other direction.

Union Station, Los Angeles (the Reagan Years)

So often the man scraped to bits by his latest try at walking
through daylight trails sheet music from a pocket, as if the
song forever dribbling from his mouth has origins in the
world. He stands too close to the tracks, though the porter
is gentle with him, guides him behind the broad yellow line
on the platform by touching softly the one elbow unexposed
(the other scabbed and bruised blue, the shirtsleeve frayed
and flapping in the easy wind blowing up from the tunnels).

The problem is the way sunlight slips through holes in the
evening air, the sound it makes, like a child choking on
water. Union Station never closes, though three times a day
it's swept two ways: a man on a rider broom motoring
through the tunnels, swerving over bottles and paper nap-
kins; the transit cops nudging to life each sleeping pile of
rags and plastic sacks, shooing them through the tall tiled
archways toward the parking lot, toward the alleys off
Oliveras Street, the 6th Street underpass, to Chinatown or
City Hall, the fenced yards beneath the Hollywood or
Harbor or Santa Monica Freeways.

It hurts to climb from dreams and shave and dress, to work
all day and wait for rush hour to end, to meet Tom and Bob
and Jeff and Dwayne in Little Tokyo for a drink before din-
ner, another after. And then to Al's Bar near the tracks: the
Blasters on at ten, the Plimsouls at twelve. The night ends
late and everyone is tired but trying not to say so, just walk-
ing slowly in the early morning emptiness of Los Angeles,
wondering if it's time to give it up and go home.

We'd known him in college: he stood in the drip of a rusted
drain pipe somewhere east of Al's, took off his shirt and
smiled. "Hey, guys," he said. "Long time no see, etcetera."

It's where you find it: public policy and smaller govern-
ment, the trickle down effect, a gray face recently excavated,
all those years of thinking it's enough, hard work and
straight dealing, all those years lifted like dust from an arti-
fact, the wind a soft brush across the lips. And then the rain
of rusty water, memory: part agent, part solvent, breaking
down to bone the irretrievable, the stripped and bruised-
through, the shame. "I'm taking a slow shower," he said.
"Now please..." he turned around and spoke over one shoul-
der. We were looking for my car. I'd parked it somewhere
near the station. "Please," he said again. "Could I have
some privacy?"

Twilight at the Edge of the Empire

Los Angeles

Each afternoon at four the winds turn east
and gently, like a barber's brush against
a neck, lift the half-ruined air and sweep
it far into the desert. The evenings
are a second chance. The foothills lean against
the sky pink and wrinkled, as sunset sweeps
the shadows from the canyons, sweeps the evening
to the sea. It seems a bruise is spreading east.
By now the plates, the silverware, are cleared;
a stain of sunlight lingers in the palms.
We light the candles and lean into our palms.
The evenings are a second chance to clear
away the strange regret, or worse, the fear
that all the day has left us with is hope.

TWO: L.A. AFTERGLOW

The city may begin from a marketplace, a trading post, the confluence of waters, but it secretly depends on the human need to walk among strangers.

−E.L. Doctorow

L.A. Afterglow

1. The Invention of Los Angeles

Remember the swallows
returning year after year
to an empty church just to find
one March that the emptiness
was complete: the church,
the town, the whole damn coast
gone? And the missionaries,
who rode north on mules
from Mexico to find a home
for the miserable angels—
those who'd failed or fallen
or given up—they named the land
for the saints: Francis to the north,
James to the south. The earth
shifted and cracked, and when
the moon found itself
stranded in a late afternoon sky
(when the light was silver instead of gold),
it was possible to watch the indigent—
their singed feathers, their bruised
and smoke-stained faces—to watch
them stagger from caves in the foothills
in the aftershock's quietude
as the dust settled on the yucca,
on the leaves of river oaks, in the shadows
of the canyon walls . . . the angels
followed the arroyos down
to the sea, took their lessons
while listening to the waves,
the easy hiss and collapse of water
reaching forth, drawing away.

2. Santa Monica Pier

In whatever was vague the light settled,
though it was torn a bit, humming with filth.
"If I had a gun," she said
but that was all or all that was audible
in the open air, the salt wind slicing
her words from her lips and to pieces,
scattering them on the wooden planks.
She spoke to another woman, slightly older,
while a boy no taller than a fire hydrant
chased after her words with a brown
paper sack. Or rather,
he ran after a handful of bait
he'd somehow dropped,
the anchovies wriggling and bouncing
like fingers of mercury.
And in their tiny bones was mercury.
She wore a blue baseball cap,
her hair a lump beneath it, and when she caught up
with her little boy near the end of the pier—
his screams so very much like
laughter, the anchovies back in the bag—
she seemed to be dusting the evening light
from his clothes, from his hair,
his cheeks. She dusted one cheek hard,
then the other.

3. *The Ruined Air*

"No recess today," said the sisters.
So we lay on our backs
beneath the grey acoustic tiles
of the music room listening
to the Singing Nun or Trini Lopez
though we weren't allowed to sing along.
"Just sip the air," said the nurse
on hand to watch us breathe.

A Stage Four alert,
the streets as still as the aftermath
of a dull sermon,
just the stirring of restless doves
beneath the eaves
or was it the old and asthmatic
gasping at the latches
of locked dormers, sealed casements?

But even then we knew
a loveliness would end it all,
sunset sizzling with lavenders and reds,
colors too vivid for nature.
And as the sky darkened
from a dusty blue to grey—
no promise of stars
in the light-soaked sky—

a long thin line of pink
stained the edge of the world,
the afterglow of ozone,
the color of a teenager's first
bikini or a flower power sticker
peeling from a bumper,
a slender neon warning
in the bruised Los Angeles sky.

4. *Foothills, Fire*

It is early August, a few weeks after
my father's 28th birthday. In the hills
above his parish a cinder has come to rest

after a long ride on the wind: a Santa Ana
from the desert, hot and dry as the breath of a lizard.
The cinder was once the live ash of a cigarette

dropped from the window of a '58 Rambler
winding up the Angeles Crest Highway—
an itinerant life insurance salesman

taking the pass through the mountains,
heading for Victorville and his next appointment.
The bloom of flame when the cinder takes root

is like a thousand poppies blown to pieces
in the wind, their gold petals thickening in the air
like the wings of migrating butterflies,

the Monarchs of Morro Bay.
But this is Los Angeles, the foothills north
of Altadena. My father can see the smoke

from his office next to the church and
there is nothing he can do. So he watches
the fire move toward Eaton Canyon,

hopes his friend John Sanders is hosing down
the roof. My mother arrives straight from
the supermarket, the Falcon idling

in the parking lot, air conditioner blasting,
frozen T.V. dinners on the back seat.
She is a few minutes early

to pick up my sisters, who are playing
in the church nursery downstairs, stops in
to say hello to my father. She starts to point

through the window at the foothills
but he is suddenly behind her,
taking the vestment off the hook on the door

as he shuts it, laying the black cloak
on the floor. She laughs and lets him
unzip her skirt, all the while watching

the fire spread through the hills
as he pulls the pins from her hair,
pulls her blouse over her head.

She can see the orange flames
when the wind gusts, the smoke lifting
for a second like a blanket shaken out

above a bed, how it drops back softly
trapping darkness and an inch of air.
The smoke billows and moves like a glacier's

dark doppelganger. And she knows the ash
will settle everywhere, that for a week
she'll wipe down the furniture, wash the car,

that her hair will darken with it
as she moves through the mornings,
the strangely gray afternoons.

Having never felt the heat, the ash
will be all she knows of the fire, a memory
that wipes clean each day and returns the next,

though there is less as the week wears on.
Until one day: nothing. Even the memory
gone. Like the marriage that will end

in twelve years, the fire will fade and then vanish;
it will seem like it never was. And finally
the foothills will come back: the long grass

and sage, the chaparral at the edge
of the arroyo. But before that, a first son.
They will name him James for her father

and a saint. She feels her husband move
inside her, the gentle collapse as he finishes
and settles on her chest like a coroner's white sheet.

She knows he will rise soon, stand up and turn,
face the mountains as he always does, every day,
whether she's there or not, looking

for something in the distance, for a sign
above the smog line. And today
he sees it: a tongue of flame through the smoke.

5. *The Dodgers, 1958*

There were no peacocks on the lawns. No angels in the palm trees.

The ravine was filled with a litter of houses, most of them
    tar paper
and cinder block, though here and there a lucky terra cotta roof
    rose above an accident
of bougainvillea, an arbor beyond a blue wall.

Down the hill in the middle distance: Chinatown, City Hall.
The children chased an old tire with a stick
as if pursuing an unattainable cliche.

A front porch rotted beneath *abuela*, the Chevys parked
    on the grass.
There were no peacocks on the lawns. No angels.

The young men in dusty fedoras (John Fante, Bukowski, the recent
Hollywood arrivals looking for work) crossed easily at the lights,
dodging out of habit the ghosts of streetcars on Wilshire Boulevard.

While in Brooklyn, trolleys rang down to silence, replaced by
    subways, fleets of taxis.

As always, the money drifted toward the ocean, to Pacific Palisades,
    Malibu.

And so O'Malley looked elsewhere: the cheap real estate east
    of town,
Mt. Washington, the Monterey Hills.

Then he moved the Mexicans out of Chavez Ravine
to make room for a home team.

6. *Airlight*

Beseechments begin with certainties:
that there is no one left to love; that the desert
has drifted inward to steady us
like salt packed in a viscera for the long journey
to the afterlife; that the deep marine canyon
between Los Angeles and Catalina
has filled with light, the cephalopods
and lantern fish dazzled nearly
to death in their blindness; that nothing—
pure nothing—is the glove of shadow
cast by a frond. And so
the airlight at dawn in the clean streets
of San Marino thins the surface of an instant
until it cracks like varnish
and the emptiness beneath is released.
In the history of the color blue
a page has been left blank for this:
the way the yellow light of the underworld
stains the sky. The man standing in the steam
says, *If only, if ever, if instead.*
And the common prayer begins, *Please, no weather,*
no temblors in the bones of the night.
Ten months without anything but light:
a drought; a desert.
Two months of rain and the levees are broken
promises, the old farms flooded,
the chimneys and rooftops an archipelago
of faith where once was certainty.
On the clean streets of Pasadena
a boy too young to care can't bear
to let the sticky lollipop lie on the sidewalk,
picks it up, begins to lick. In other words
it's normal, even if it hurts: the sickness
beneath a footstep; the light dissolved in flood;
the crime instead of hope; the poppies springing
from ash in the aftermath of this year's fires.

7. *Border Radio*

"50,000 watts out of Mexico"
          –Dave Alvin

In Redlands, beneath the I 10 overpass
on Colton Avenue,
on spring Sundays in 1981,
in the El Burrito parking lot,
my brother Tom and I laid beach towels
in the back of his Datsun pickup
and hid the cooler in the cab
where we could reach it through the open window.
We split a number 10 (beef, bean and rice burrito
with a side of guacamole)
and turned on the radio loud enough
to hear above the trucks passing overhead,
the Macks and Peterbilts leaving L.A. empty
or struggling in from Arizona with loads
so heavy the concrete-wrapped girders
creaked like bed springs.
But with the knob twisted right
we could hear the accordion and guitar, the four-part harmonies
of a wedding song, some celebration
of love lifting like mown grass in a wind
through smog and the first heat of spring.
We drank Bohemia and listened
to the border radio, Mexican music riding the waves
up the Imperial Valley through all
the old mission towns on 15, towns crowded now
by stucco subdivisions, the groves giving way
to suburban lawns, those strange
squares of green we wonder over
from airplanes heading east, since west is nothing
but ocean and sky, the blue over blue
of Diebenkorn, horizon at sea, an argument of blue.
If we parked the Datsun just right
the truck was a Japanese antenna
picking up the last of those 50,000 watts.

We'd listen for hours, our shirts off,
catching rays and a good beer buzz until Señor Fernandez
pulled down the shutters on the take-out window
and dragged a stool and a guitar out from behind
his taqueria. And each Sunday evening
that spring of '81, he sang us *"Solamente Una Vez,"*
a song "as cheesy as they come" my friend Hector
would later tell me. But Señor Fernandez
loved a love song, and he sang each one
as if he'd written it for his wife, who banged pots
and threw trash bags out the back door
as if to let us know she was watching.
"El corazon grande," Señor Fernandez always said to us
thumping his chest. Then he'd crack
the seal on a new pint of Cuervo
and pass it to Tom.
On clear evenings the signal grew stronger
as the sun sank somewhere off Santa Monica,
and we lay in the back of the truck
until the two or three stars strong enough to shine
blinked on in the L.A. sky.
Only then did the station start its sad songs,
which Señor Fernandez knew as well,
songs about home and about leaving it,
the distant north, the endless fields.
Sometimes his wife came out to get him
but usually he sang until he cried there beneath the freeway,
until Tom and I said we had to go.
He'd take the Bohemia we always offered
and hide it under the neck of the guitar in its case,
then walk toward the screen door
where his wife waited, slapping
tortillas back and forth between her hands,
watching the sky and her husband
and the two foolish *gringos*, listening herself
to the transistor radio on the stove, to the same sad songs
her husband knew by heart.

8. East of Los Angeles, 1992

When last the city burned
and you, my lonely father, described
the smoke riding the afternoon breeze
as a bank of dirty fog heading for the hills,
a soiled handkerchief looking for a pocket . . .
when you called the smoke
a cloud in the canyon, "just a cloud,"
I was old enough at last to know
it wasn't true
and still believe you.

9. Surf City

It's clear that no one is left in the green room
of a breaking wave. I drove for years
from Long Beach to San Clemente looking
for the clean left shoulders
of a south swell, my arm tossed
around the Queen of California.
And though I loved her, she wore nothing
but a needle trail, a track of blue nickels,
as if each touch in her life had left a bruise. A breeze
across the beach is the clean air
of the past; it lifts just enough litter and
grit to slice the soft skin beneath an eye.
Cartoon balloons float above the sleeping sun bathers,
the comfortably poor leaking easily from surf shops
and bungalows, wondering if, in fact, it is all
ladders propped against walls, no way out but under.
It seems the water is not quite fine
to swim in, though please, let us bathe ourselves
and the children and take the pill that keeps us well,
paddle beyond the surf line in the dust light of
afternoon's departure, the California of my past circa
1968, when even Bobby Kennedy couldn't bear to leave,
his peace a sleep of the just, to some a sort of justice.
I knew Sirhan Sirhan's mother, who lived one street over
on El Molino and said nothing when we returned
the borrowed cookie sheet filled with lemon squares,
just stared past us at a pair of rusty chains hanging
from the linden. Her son spends his days
in San Quentin signalling the ships off shore,
their holds filled with the broken timbers
of recovered wrecks, with all we will need
to build anew in the new age, in the aftermath.

10. Afterthought: The Bends

The smoke in the foothills
is a canyon speaking spanish
to the sky: chaparral and manzanita,
the oil in their roots and leaves
igniting in the thick syllables
of July, ash in drifts
by the curb. A car starts,
a cough, a flock of doves
lifting from the husk
of a dried-out date palm.
Dawn light and dusk light
move toward each other
like remnants of conversation,
an argument passing into
noise as it leaks from a window.
And so an old star
lets loose its dust
and it sizzles like grease
on its way through time,
lodges like a shard
in the hollow pockets of our bones,
in the blood bubbling in the joints
as we rise too fast to catch
our breath, to reach
the air of other worlds, to leave
the smoke of a sacked city.

THREE: EAST

. . . To
you I offer my hull and the tattered cordage
of my will. The terrible channels where
the wind drives me against the brown lips
of the reeds are not all behind me. Yet
I trust the sanity of my vessel; and
if it sinks, it may well be in answer
to the reasoning of the eternal voices,
the waves which have kept me from reaching you.

–*Frank O'Hara*
from "To the Harbormaster"

California Stars in West Virginia (for Walt)

"I want to rest my heavy head tonight
On a bed of California stars,
I want to lay my weary bones tonight
On a bed of California stars."

–Woody Guthrie

The almond orchard behind Caroline's house
is cross-hatched with roads
that seem to lead away to somewhere
east of everything: the Sierras, the clouds
above them, the last lost lake in America.
In spring the earth is furred
with grass beneath the trees,
which bud snowflakes and fresh
handkerchiefs, the long gone white of almond blossoms.
At night in a new moon's broken beam it seems
the stars have decided to give all their light
to a single hour; the flowers
are singed by starlight; they are bursting into flames
so cool the air for miles
is edged with frost.

Walt slept once in a pram by Carrie's pool
in March and woke covered with blossoms;
I found him gently chewing one,
his hair aged by flowers, the receiving blanket embroidered
with almond petals.
Three years later he asked why the starlight felt like
soft fingers on his cheeks,
like flowers, he said.
We were in the backyard watching
the night settle in the privet, a night too warm
to worry the fading annuals;
I was grilling steaks and he was helping,

his plastic tongs, his white chef's hat.
Walt remembered nothing of spring in the San Joaquin,
of driving through orchards hung loosely
with mist, the smell of water in the ditches, the moon
a white hole in the aqueduct, stars
freckling the irrigation puddles.
"Like flowers," he said again as I imagined the almond
blossoms, as I turned to watch a firefly
settle easily on Walt's cheek,
a firefly with nothing to fear in the falling dusk, the little boy
looking for stars, feeling the light on his face.

The Seminary Commencement

Someone in line ahead of me
is buying bread and a can of milk.
She is whispering to her friend,
"Don't tell a soul" and her friend
is nodding slowly and gazing off
past the checker, the bagger,
the festooned windows of
the supermarket, as if the secret
is a small hill on the horizon
she can just see now, just barely.
Has she learned how to make
a meal from bread and sweet milk?
Or is the private truth less domestic,
less useful, a loose thread of gossip
she can carry in her pocket, worry
with her fingertips. Outside
in West Virginia the seventeen-year
secret is being told, the cicadas
unburying themselves to sing
their two notes to the trees,
to taste the leaves. And in the country
of California my father, at 66,
is receiving his doctorate on a hot
June day, is listening to the dithyrambs
beyond the sermon: the bamboo
ghosting the stained glass windows
and shaking its dry husks; the row
of eucalyptus along the road, a wind break
with so many ways of saying one thing:
"there is a breeze in my leaves."
In the church above the freeway
he is remembering how the foothills
seem to wear the cloud shadows
like capes, how orange blossoms in spring
turn mornings into rooms of women,

the dust of scented water hanging in the air.
I'm next in line with a package of cheese,
a dozen eggs and two cookies
for my little boy, who reaches past
my fingers as they sort dollars
and slips one cookie free of the bag.
My father is taking the diploma
in one hand, is bending down
for the hood. And as he shakes
hands with the seminary president
he hears the traffic on Lake Avenue,
the distant murmur of the freeway.
And then the doves rustling
palm fronds, the quiet small talk
of his congregation filing past, the bell.
It could be they are ringing a bell
for the ceremony, a graduation
commemoration, but he knows
it's a memory, the sound the wind
makes when it has traveled two miles
and thirty years carrying the clap
of tongue on iron. His congregation
is scattered or dead, the doves
glow a spectral white in the window
above Mary. But if he listens closely
he can hear instead my son, who has
my pant leg in his fist and is asking
for the other cookie.

Never Mind

You were my first in all ways.
You covered your mouth when you laughed.
I saw you cry so rarely that knowing now
how often you cried is a razor's clean revision.
We were sixteen together, and seventeen.
And then, later, every few months, you'd send a letter
where I learned where you'd moved, what the work
was like, who you'd seen in a supermarket, how you cried.
There was a pact, a particular year when we'd meet again,
the day after your birthday, a phone call
I would make. When I heard what happened
I was thinking of someone else, a new person
I shouldn't love, would like to love, am not allowed to love.
And as is true so often, no one else knew: I was
trying to get it wrong again, succeeding.
And instead of you or her, my girlfriend phoned
to say, *What is it with you*, to say, *Never mind*,
which is what I'd been doing. And then we said nothing,
though we didn't hang up. The silence stretched between us
along roads and rivers, from phone pole
to phone pole, through circuits and switches:
a line man found his hands going numb;
the birds lifted off the wires
in fear or disgust, then fell in waves
like dissipated noise, took cover in the tall grass.
Take cover. *Never mind me*, she said, a phrase
instead of nothing, the gentle hiss of distance dissolving.
You'd had a child, nearly died giving birth. When my mother
called she couldn't tell me. Then she told me. She said,
She almost died, and her voice caught before finishing,
like a leaf snagged in a fence waiting for the wind,
for a chance to keep falling. And I remembered
when all my mistakes could fit in your small hands,
how you cupped my face like a handful of water,
then let it go.

By Heart

October. The year begins to forget itself
in ceremony and smoke,
the cedar chests open
to sweet smelling clothes,
invitations embossed
with leaves, leaves
lifting from drifts
and covering the parked cars.
After the opera, the dinner dance, the ball,
the river fills
with long, white gloves
and cummerbunds, carnations and swollen corks,
the programs creased
like toy boats,
reckless remains
of moments grown thick
with the eternal.
The hostess wears
a sleek mask of feathers, her face
worn thin as paper,
nearly torn beside the lips.
There is candle light,
cool air. October:
silver flasks in hip pockets.
The tailgates open
to casseroles, kegs of beer. At dusk
the stadiums empty. A few stragglers,
the plastic sacks,
the sifting of garbage for loose cans.
Through windows on the walk home
the glow of kitchens, the kettles of soup.
The first shards
of headache behind the eyes, scores flashing
on the screen, a friend nursing a last drink
as the weekend

folds its arms across its chest.
And the months ahead narrow into belief
and a bitter loneliness;
how very cruel faith seems
to the faithless, how light the wrapped package
that is given by heart alone.
A thin, stray wind
down the chimney fills the room
with smoke. October.
All is foolish except honor and love.
The children in costume. And the long nights begin.

Winter Memory of Summer Trespass

Somewhat lovelier than snow,
a piece for four hands, the light
slips loose of evening
as furnace currents soft as summer curtains
rock the hanging fern.

The ficus has frozen on the sun porch,
forecasts of frost ignored; the rolled hose
by the door is a rope of coiled ice;
an August memory
is cracking in the cold.

If it never happened
then how has it fixed itself
like steam to a wet window?
You kissed me without warning,
without wondering why you wanted to.

It was a weekend at the shore;
we were friends waiting
for other friends to arrive;
it was nothing; I said, *Please, no.*
It was the week before

the week your gentle drift into loss ended
at loss. At Payne Whitney
you watched from a window the trucks
back into docks where grown men in gloves
moved crates onto dollies and rolled

the innumerable dear items into the long
warehouses near the river.
("The lovely river," you wrote,
"how it flashes its string of knives.")
You watched the cabs

disgorge their passengers
(the brightly feathered birds)
into a wing-clipped world stunned
to stumbling by perfect weather.
As summer passed into rumor

you healed halfway, as if settling
for a house near the shore, the breezes
swollen with the smells of seaweed
and salt, a province south of happiness.
And when last we spoke—

a phone call between
phone calls—you swore it never happened,
the body held not holding back, the bruise
you gave me, a kiss so wrong it left a stain.
"Is it snowing, where you are?" you said,

"has it started to snow?"
Three blocks from the breath
behind your voice, I watched the wind
thicken, the darkness etched with blown flakes.
"Not yet," I said. "Wait a minute. Yes."

Mother to Daughter

Each regret, like a sweater
or scarf, finds its nail in the wind.
Just as light puddles in the stalled moments
of an evening stroll, when she remembers how easily
her mother swept the petals off the table,
crushed them in her palm, pulled her blouse
away from her chest, sprinkled the dried rose
between her breasts.
  And now she helps her
find her place in a book, her bent glasses
in the butter dish, the inexplicable framed photograph
beneath a sofa cushion. She had hoped, always hoped
to hear this: the thank yous, the soft
endearments.
  But how could she know
her mother's lapse into tenderness
could hurt so bad? And now she's trying to tell me
but she can't, just can't, her fingers talking,
sewing the air with the last few sentences
she can't say.
  I won't help her
hate herself; I'm here to open a window.
To hold her inside as everything she's known
rushes out into the garden
to take its place beside her mother,
who's on her knees in the earth, digging up
the bulbs she planted yesterday.

Instead of Nothing

Privately there was hope. Elizabeth's hands
began to open again, and one day, without
display or knowing, she lifted
the glass of water to her ear
as if listening to a small sea.
I called the doctor, on holiday at the shore,
who smiled at the news, or at least
it sounded so.
Lovely, he said.

~

Her first words were, "No, never,"
though she spoke them to a pot of mums.
The sunlight on the brick patio
was broken by the elm's blue shade.
I rolled her wheelchair gingerly in and out
of the shadows as if they were burning,
the crumbling lilac dropping its gray blossoms
like piles of ash. Each morning I read to her,
cut the cantaloupe into bites she might
accept. Each day I tried out a new name,
Emily or Eugenia, Evelyn, Estelle.
Perhaps she had caught like a cold
someone else's memory,
a different road down into darkness,
her own as lost as the air in a dream,
sharp and unbreathable.

~

This is how it happened:
I pulled the steering wheel left to miss the deer
and we spun slowly, like the hands
of a clock in an old film,
how the spurned lover is not yet

aware of his loss, waiting
with roses outside the Plaza Hotel,
watching the carriages vanish
into Central Park as the camera
cuts away, to the clock
in Grand Central Station,
its hands spinning,
just as we spun toward the median,
the soft grass and wildflowers.
But we never got there.
And when the brand new Buick
slammed into us Elizabeth
was facing me, turned toward me
as if to respond to a question,
as if listening attentively,
though, in fact, she just
didn't want to watch it happen.
When it all stopped, when we were finally
still, the Buick's polished grill
was where she had been sitting,
though I could see her in the distance,
lying on the grass;
she seemed to be watching the clouds.
The wind through the windshield
dried the blood on my hands, lifted
the smallest flecks of glass
and blew them away.

~

Years ago, one evening, before
any of this, I found her
in the side yard. She had pulled a plastic
lawn chair around the house
and sat smoking by herself,
a seashell in her left hand where she ashed
the cigarette. She hadn't wanted me to see,
the old habit resumed. And the two
together, her need and its corresponding shame
were ways of saying, "There are things I can't forget,"

though earlier, while peppering the salad,
she'd paused to sip her wine, to tell me
she'd forgiven me. She held up her hand
when I tried to speak, when I tried to promise.

~

She looks away now as I curl back her fingers,
watches a robin bothering the underbrush
near the fence, seems to notice a tuft of grass
between the flagstones.
She is almost ready to speak, to say
Stupid bird, or, Spring.
I light a cigarette, cough,
tighten her fingers around it.
I sit with the folded newspaper across the patio
and watch the smoke rise around her face,
a face so empty and still it seems
engraved in ivory, a locket stuck shut.
The ash lengthens and withers, falls into her lap,
but she doesn't drop the cigarette.
At any moment she might begin
to smoke, to remember why she started
hating me once so long ago, that other history
I'd hoped to forget, that I would
now accept gratefully instead of nothing.
When the cigarette begins to burn her fingers
I lean forward to slap it loose
but she holds on; she balls her hand
into a fist around that small dot of fire.
I remember how my father used to
swallow his lighted cigarette, a parlor trick.
I hold her left hand and wait
for the right hand to open.

Midwinter Visitant

The boy has forgotten his socks again.
Cold settles in drifts
around his ankles,
the tongue-in-groove floors
bare but for a brief carpet of dust.
His father is not home.
His mother is in the attic retrieving a quilt.
Downstairs in the window seat, he is waiting
because he wants to see it again; there is just
one more chance before his mother says, *Now*
and bedtime begins, the hour or so
of brushing teeth and hearing
stories, the tucking in,
the soft singing.
He will be alone all night
and soon, a night too long to fill completely
with sleep, the cold so vivid beyond
the walls—the house banked by drifts of snow—
his blood will freeze, he is certain, in the small sack
of his body. He has forgotten his socks,
the thick pair his mother left at the foot
of his bed; his hair
is wet from the bath; the front window
faces the street, is smoked with frost.
He can hear his mother say
his name, say, *Where are you?*
and now she is coming down the stairs
as he watches and waits.

The streetlamp drops its light
into the snow; there are no cars, no people walking home.
His mother is on the landing, she can see
him now, can see he's forgotten
his socks, she is about
to say, *Now*.

He watches the street for it,
his forehead pressed against the glass—
he can hear the tick of snow settling
in the basement window wells,
the gentle hum
of the streetlamp.
Now, she says
as it rounds the corner, *Right now*
as it moves into a gallop, the piebald mare
that *Isn't there,* his father says,
There isn't a horse for miles,
though it runs past the house
through the falling light, the faint blur
of flurries just beginning,
the snow-dust that ages all that is motionless,
limns the cars and trash cans
in soft grays and vague whites, fills
the tire tracks and footprints,
the scalloped hollows of hooves,
until the trail of presence
is unprovable, just a whisper
stranded in a child's mouth.

When the Circus Comes

She liked my circus poem best,
though she could never remember the title.
She once held an early draft up to the window
as if examining a palimpsest; I think she'd noticed
the line of hers I'd pinched. She leaned back
in her chair and said, "Harmsy, this is good."
Another time, after I'd fallen asleep on a front lawn
the night before, I called and she said,
"Just drink some O.J. and have a shower. Then wait.
You'll feel better by dinner. I should know."
My favorite circus poem is Kenneth Koch's second one,
especially the part where he mentions his first one,
which I've never read. What I mean is he has two poems
called "The Circus," and talks about the one in the other.
Mine is not called "The Circus," though she called it
my circus poem. Los Lobos have a terrific song on *Kiko* that goes,
"That day I'll burn this whole place down,
when the circus comes to town." But someone's
leaving in that song—I guess someone's always leaving—
and the circus is about arrival. It's like a rip at the knee
of your blue jeans: when you start out for work in the morning
it's a slight tear—a few pegs scattered around, rope and canvas
        in piles—
but by evening there's a yawning mouth the size of your knee,
        the bigtop
filling the vacant lot next to the Texaco. And if
you go or if you don't, if you buy the ticket
from the wheel or stay home, the elephants sound the same;
they sound better than they look, to be honest.
There's nothing sadder than a small time pachyderm.
Like a traveling salesman's scarred valise—you wince a little
watching it bob down the street toward you;
you know you're going to be asked to see it for what
it isn't: exotic and wild, filled with cures and dreams and wishes.

And the stakes being pulled from the ground, they woosh
like a screen door settling shut. The llama nips
the camel's tail as it follows him up the ramp into the truck.
The key is to leave before you're missed, to leave in darkness.
She left town, left the road, left me wondering what to call it
when the circus leaves too early.

In Any Country

an Epithalamium

Rain in a wine glass left on the window sill.
It's noon, she's making coffee, a sheet wrapped around her
    shoulders.
She knows which song is next on the record, begins to sing softly.
He is half-sleeping on the sofa, humming "Harborcoat"
into the sleeve of his robe, his face
striped with sunlight through half-closed blinds.

She remembers summer somewhere else, a fountain,
a square in the center of a city:
the folding wooden chairs, the old men in heavy shoes, black
    jackets
over their arms, playing cards or taking sun.
She is dancing with him though there isn't any music,
the gazebo empty, the band still asleep, music trapped in
    their minds. . . .
And their dancing is a small act of public recklessness,
like spilling coffee on a white tablecloth.
Still, the crowd, the passersby, they turn to stare . . . at love, perhaps,
or its expression, the casual twirl, a body folded in arms.
An old man begins to whistle to their movements.

She sips her coffee, slides the glass door west.
The music rises, crows from a clothesline.
She moves out onto the balcony to feel the day, to a triangle
of sunlight at the far corner; she puts her hands in it.
He is waiting in the kitchen, cutting limes, two glasses
    rimmed with salt.
And the shape two figures make embracing
is a horizon of hills reflected in water.

June

I think it was that woman's laughter
that reminded me of our need to know,
so clear it is that she doesn't know
what her companion thinks of her, how he leans
into her laugh and touches his wine glass
without lifting it. If I believe in you we may
receive their dinners by mistake, a form
of prayer in some cultures, where the random
arrival of food is as freighted with hope as the Tarot.
Or is it the small sprig of something she wears pinned
to her pocket that makes me think of Blake,
his habit of covering lunch stains with funny buttons?
He died in 1982, though for years I pretended differently,
scratching my cheek as he did when considering
the angle in billiards. His mother named him for
the mystic, not the poet, as if we all have two
closets to consult each morning. But today
is my birthday, May 20th, a Saturday,
and you are treating me to dinner at dusk and al fresco,
our favorite restaurant, our favorite spot at the edge
of the patio. The bees are wrestling above the garden tables,
bouncing and dodging, thumping each other like drunk lovers,
buzzing the bright blouse of that lovely little girl
who seems ready to scream, her mother waving
a white napkin. These evenings are fragrant
with summer, you can taste it at the edge of each breath.
Like fog lifting from a freshly planted field, how it arrives
at your window redolent of loam, it seems we are
in the doorway waiting for the sounds of lawnmowers
and window fans, for the air to thicken with heat.
But then time really is a distance as they say,
and if we hurry we'll get somewhere by morning,
perhaps June. Let me help you with your salad.
I'd wear a suit out of season (the sandy linen one
with the backward pleats) if I thought it would

carry us through "the charity of the hard moments."
But it seems at any second the rain will be
loosening our buttons, and it is not
so much a sinecure that I propose but a little
laughter in the face of it. I forget it isn't you
grown quiet in the green light spilling through
strange trees, but my memory of you.
We were talking about Blake. Loss is the province
next door to presence, you say. Well, yes, I suppose.
But what about who I was before, the strange shoes
I wore? And that vague beauty hidden in the folds
of a silk shirt packed away, the arms trapped behind,
the fumes of camphor—I could call it hope,
it was that sweet—do I leave it behind as well?
Oh but it's learning to live with loss, they say,
that will burnish the slim remains, though with what
it isn't written. As if we had so much more.
As if we hadn't given most of it away.
I had meant to tell you about Blake
the first time we made love (forgive me
for forgetting), but I was listening to what
you were saying. And suddenly I thought of
the wine in the refrigerator, the strawberries:
how easily summer heals, whether bought
in small baskets or simply remembered.
So why won't you let him go, you say.
Let him go, yes. It's funny but I once imagined you
in feather boas, nothing else. And though often termed
a struck reverie, I find wonder an uncoiling,
how they slipped from your shoulders,
snaked around your hips. But I have nothing
to fear for this never happened; I can let it go.

As the heavy mist this morning left its fingerprints
on the porch swing, the past is a rash
that now and then recurs; and I don't want
to cure it. But could we have that wine now?
I know Blake would approve of this armistice,
this supposition of love, and Blake was my first friend
to leave early, I listen to him.

Sleek for the Long Flight

W.M.

Rain in quick eighth notes
made Broadway a brief
song, the shower passing
east into Queens
like a curtain drawn back.
The taxi was humid
with breath and
the heat from our hair:
Paige and Noelle
on either side of me,
David by the driver,
you giving directions
as you leaked
cigarette smoke out
the inch of open window.
You'd only heard
about the restaurant,
a silly hybrid of Tex-Mex
and Italian, ethnic dining
run amok on the Upper
West Side. And you couldn't
promise anything, though later,
not even the strange
confusion of food
could sap your love of what
was hidden there,
the three or four stray
herbs in the salad,
something wrong
with the sauce that made it
different, you said,
and almost good.

Aubade in Morgantown

The garbage men wake me at dawn
as they back their truck into place,
though they're whispering, passing
the cans above their heads.

From your bathroom window
the rooftops are tangled in the flat, gray air,
antennae listing in broken ranks, lawn chairs
leaning against dormers.

The college students are sleeping
who sun themselves afternoons
on their pitched roofs. The neighbors'
walled garden is quiet as a caught breath,

though from your bathroom window
we (and only we) can see the bricks
fanned between plots of daisies
and petunias, their outdoor shower

without curtain or door, the smoldering
rhododendron, its purple petals
like bruised skin lit from within. Only we
can watch them make love

on their plastic furniture in the moonlight.
Down the hall I find you still asleep
in a drone of fans, one propped
against a stack of books, the other

roaring in the window. I unwind
the sheet from your leg, cover
the rest of you, lick your neck below the ear
so that you smile without waking.

And without waking you I leave
though I've forgotten something necessary,
my wallet or a laundry ticket, something
I'll need later, that I will return for.

Want

I want nothing more than this:

to hear the blood in your hands when they touch my face;
to listen at the edge of sleep to your breath grown steady;
to fix the torn hem in your favorite dress before you return
    from a day of errands;
to never seek your notice of the small ways, the slight repairs
    of love;
to sear red peppers on a grill, the strips of steak, to pour the drinks
    and hear through the kitchen window the phone ring,
    your laughter;
to love from a distance as you laugh;
to fear truthfully, like a sparrow in the dark weeds, instead
    of hopelessly as I do when your image, for whole seconds,
    flickers loosely and vanishes, my mind a lit theatre,
    the film on fire;
to smile quietly when your back is turned, because it isn't time yet
    to say it again;
to ache a little less in your absence;
to feel the hush that follows rain as silence and not a figure for loss;
to find your fingerprints in the soil of a house plant, to fill them
    with water;
to want for all things but not for you;
to know my wanting is a way of holding;
to hold without hurting;
to leave the windows open, to find a room filled with pear
    blossoms, to leave them there for days, to find them
    in your hair.

The Sanity of My Vessel

You're never here but here
you are, and you're smiling, a pair
of pink slippers hooked to your fingers.

If this were a dream
a small door would open in your body,
swallows would not be lost

in their migratory myths (they clatter
in the cold chimney as if
their blood remembers).

You are not a dream, a ghost,
an apparition, but you have risen
from the dust of a deep corner

because you are not here and here
is all I have. So I am readying the horses,
sewing a tear in my blue coat.

For it is nearly over,
the quiet of seaglass and sand,
a quiet that fills

instead of empties, the blown snow
finding the crack in the porch door.
The silence is slipping like a tongue

into sound, and I am almost to the gate,
almost ready to depart.
Repaired of dress and listening for how

the trees in reaching down to scratch
the bony rooftops recall your weary sigh,
my lighthouse, my siren (please wait),

I am very nearly on my way.

Notes

"Western Sky" borrows its title and central metaphor from two different songs by Mark Eitzel.

The epigraph to "California Stars in West Virginia (for Walt)" is credited to Woody Guthrie, who wrote the words, though the song "California Stars" is performed by the band Wilco, whose members wrote the music.

The penultimate line in "By Heart" comes from James Salter and can be found in his memoir *Burning the Days*.

"Sleek for the Long Flight" takes its title from the book by the same name by William Matthews, to whom the poem is dedicated.

"In Any Country" is for Dwayne Beck and Melissa Love, dear friends.

"Twilight at the Edge of the Empire" is for David Wojahn, with thanks.

"Loves Leaves More than Flowers" is for my sister Caroline.

"Reunion of Extra Shadows" and "June" are in memory of Blake Edwards.

"Elegy as Evening, as Exodus" and "When the Circus Comes" are in memory of Lynda Hull.

The poem "Harriet Doerr" was written while she was alive. Mrs. Doerr died November 17, 2002; I've chosen to leave the poem in the present tense.

>>>

My thanks to Gerald Costanzo, whose support has been unwavering. Thanks also to his staff at Carnegie Mellon University Press, particularly Cynthia Lamb.

Much thanks to Dean Young for his care in reading the manuscript.

For the third time, thank you Linda Warren for making a beautiful book.

And to Jeff Carpenter, my gratitude for the friendship and the fellowship, the many years of being there.

Finally, this collection would not exist in its present state without the help of Paige Muendel. The poems "Want," "Aubade in Morgantown," and "The Sanity of My Vessel" were written for her.

ABOUT THE AUTHOR

James Harms is the author of three earlier books of poetry from Carnegie Mellon University Press, Quarters, The Joy Addict *and* Modern Ocean, *as well as a limited edition, letterpress volume,* East of Avalon. *He lives with his family in Morgantown, West Virginia, where he directs the creative writing program at West Virginia University and the West Virginia Writers' Workshop.*

ABOUT THE BOOK

The text of Freeways and Aqueducts *is set in Hightower (1994), designed by Tobias Frere-Jones, and Vitrina (1996), designed by Pablo A. Medina. This book was designed by Linda Warren at Studio Deluxe, Culver City, California. It was printed and bound by Jeff Carpenter of Westcott Press, Altadena, California.*